Compassionate Love and Dementia

Caregiver's guide to
understanding Dementia
behaviors

By

Shane Raymond

All rights reserved 2023

Shane Raymond

Table of Contents

Presentation

Chapter one
Introduction
Understanding the Purpose of the Guide
The Importance of Compassionate Love in Dementia Care

Chapter two
Overview of Dementia
Treatment and care
Taking care of oneself
WHO reaction
Different Types of Dementia
Common Symptoms and Progression
Signs and side effects
Impact on the Individual and Caregiver

Chapter three
Dementia Behaviors: A Comprehensive Understanding
Agitation and Restlessness
Anxiety and Fear
Repeating and Disorientation
Sundowning and Sleep Disturbances
Wandering and Safety Concerns
Aggression and Irritability
Hallucinations and Delusions

Chapter Four
Compassionate Love and the Dementia Caregiver
Cultivating Empathy and Understanding
Nurturing Emotional Connection
Recognizing Personal Histories and Memories
Promoting Dignity and Autonomy
Self-Care for the Caregiver

Chapter five
Effective Communication Strategie
Non-Verbal Communication Technique
Active Listening and Validation
Using Visual Aids and Simple Instructions:
Reducing Distractions for Better communication

Chapter six
Creating a Nurturing Environment
Designing a Safe and Stimulating Living
Establishing Consistent Routines and Schedules
Incorporating Meaningful Activities
Incorporating Familiar Objects and Music:

Chapter seven
Managing Challenging Dementia Behaviors
Understanding the Triggers for Behaviors
Strategies for Calming Agitation and Restlessness
Tips to assist with forestalling disturbances
Dealing with Aggression and Irritability
Coping with Sundowning and Sleep Disturbances
Preventing Wandering and Ensuring Safety

Chapter eight
Seeking Professional Support and Resources
The Role of Medical Professionals in Dementia Care
Enlisting the Help of Support Groups
Counselling and Therapy for Caregivers
Assistive Devices and Technology for Dementia Care

Chapter nine
Practical Tips for Everyday Dementia Care
Assisting with Daily Living Activities
Ensuring Proper Nutrition and Hygiene
Encouraging Physical Activity and Exercise
Engaging in Meaningful Social Connections

Chapter ten
Embracing Compassionate Love: Stories from Caregiver
Real-Life Experiences and Insights
Lessons Learned from Compassionate Caregivers
Inspiring Examples of Compassionate
Love in Dementia Care

Chapter eleven
Conclusion
Recap of Key Points
10 Encouraging Quotes for Caregivers

Presentation

The quantity of individuals determined to have dementia is expanding, making a critical financial burden universal. With the movement of the infection, patients need a parental figure whose prosperity is significant for nonstop consideration.

Giving reprieve as a help, through sharing the obligation of providing care or backing for the guardian, is an expensive drive. A distributed internet-based help stage for dementia parental figures, persuaded by the sharing economy, putting trade of expertise, assets, and administrations in its middle, can possibly offset cost worries with a quest for break. The point of this examination is to survey parental figures' aim to participate in distributed trade.

Dementia guardians comprise a weak section of the general public due to the psychosocial effect of really focusing on dementia patients. Notwithstanding the actual burden as far as long periods of care are concerned, dementia guardians experience the mental degradation of friends and family, and this is a wellspring of mental trouble for them. Regulation of dementia patients isn't guaranteed to work on the prosperity of guardians, and they might be upheld during the change of insight. Supporting the parental figure during the course of casual consideration is fundamental to guaranteeing their prosperity. This has prompted a broad examination of medications for dementia caregiver figures' prosperity, going from mental conduct treatment to directing social help to rest, where rest is characterized as the empowering of brief splits from providing care liabilities.

Intercessions, for example, psychoeducation and mental social treatment somewhat diminished parental figure weight, sadness, and tension while reasonably expanding the capacity and information of the guardians. Intercessions that combine more than one methodology are viewed as more successful.

Chapter one

Introduction

Understanding the Purpose of the Guide

Really focusing on a friend or family member with dementia can be both fulfilling and testing. As a guardian, it is vital to comprehend the different ways of behaving related to dementia to give it proper consideration and backing. This guide means to reveal insight into these ways of behaving while at the same time accentuating the significance of humane love in the care-giving venture. Dementia is an umbrella term that encompasses a range of mental degradation problems.

The most well-known type of dementia is Alzheimer's disease; however, there are others, for example, vascular dementia and Lewy body dementia. No matter what the particular analysis, a wide range of dementias present unique difficulties for both the individual with dementia and their guardians. In this aide, we will investigate the multi-layered nature of dementia's ways of behaving and offer bits of knowledge into the hidden causes. By fostering an extensive comprehension of these ways of behaving, parental figures can move toward their job with sympathy, compassion, and persistence. We will dig into techniques for overseeing testing ways of behaving, upgrading correspondence, and establishing a supportive climate for their friends and family. Empathetic love lies at the core of dementia care. It includes a profound comprehension of the individual with dementia as an individual, perceiving their common history, and giving consideration that depends on regard and compassion.

This guide will underscore the significance of keeping up with profound associations and cultivating a feeling of nobility and independence for the individual with dementia. We will examine viable tips and methods to oversee normal conduct difficulties like tumult, hostility, meandering, and sundowning. By furnishing guardians with techniques that address these ways of behaving, we intend to upgrade their capacities to give significant consideration, at last working on personal satisfaction for both the parental figure and the individual with dementia. It is significant to remember that each individual's involvement in dementia is unique. While this guide can give general bits of knowledge and ideas, individual requirements and inclinations should be considered. By embracing the standards of humane love, parental figures can adjust and fit their way to deal with the particular conditions and difficulties they experience.

All in all, this guide looks to help guardians in their journey of figuring out sympathy and empathy for people with dementia. By offering pragmatic exhortation and underscoring the significance of humane love, parental figures can explore the intricacies of dementia and ways of behaving with elegance and give the most ideal consideration to their friends and family. Together, we can have a constructive outcome in the lives of those impacted by dementia.

The Importance of Compassionate Love in Dementia Care

Dementia is an ever-evolving mental confusion that influences a great many individuals around the world. As the illness advances, people with dementia frequently experience changes that can be trying for them and their guardians. To give successful consideration and understanding, it is pivotal to use humane love. Humane love envelops sympathy, figuring out, tolerance, and benevolence. It includes the capacity to interface with and care for others on a profound, close-to-home level, cultivating a feeling of having a place, solace, and security. With regards to dementia care, humane love gives an establishment to building trust and advancing prosperity in people with dementia.

Importance of Compassionate Love in Dementia Care Introduction:

1. Improves profound prosperity: Individuals with dementia frequently experience sensations of disarray, dread, and dissatisfaction. Empathetic love can assist with mitigating these feelings by giving a conviction that all is good and understanding. Guardians who approach

dementia care with merciful love establish a strong and encouraging climate, prompting close-to home prosperity for people with dementia.

2. Decreases testing ways of behaving: Dementia can appear in different testing ways of behaving, like unsettling, animosity, and opposition. These ways of behaving are often a consequence of disarray or the powerlessness to communicate needs. Empathetic love permits parental figures to really address these ways of behaving by approving feelings and giving delicate consolation. By recognizing and answering with empathy, guardians can assist with limiting testing ways of behaving and upgrading the general consideration experience.

3. Upholds individual-focused care: Humane love in dementia care requires an individual-focused approach. It perceives the uniqueness and singularity of every individual with dementia, zeroing in on their particular necessities, inclinations, and life history. By embracing humane love, parental figures can fit their consideration systems to suit the individual, advancing independence, pride, and identity worth.

4. Further develops correspondence: Dementia frequently debilitates verbal relational abilities, making it difficult for people to communicate their requirements. Humane love urges guardians to use non-verbal signs, undivided attention, and persistence while speaking with people with dementia. This approach works with better

comprehension and takes into consideration more viable correspondence, lessening dissatisfaction and improving the nature of care.

Sympathetic love assumes an imperative role in dementia care. By getting it and embracing the standards of sympathetic love, parental figures can establish a sustaining and strong climate that advances profound prosperity, lessens testing ways of behaving, upholds individual-focused care, and further develops correspondence with people with dementia.

Chapter two

Overview of Dementia

Dementia is a term for a few infections that influence memory, thinking, and the capacity to perform day-to-day exercises.
The ailment deteriorates over the long haul. It fundamentally influences more established individuals, yet not all individuals will get it as they age.

Things that increase the risk of creating dementia include:

- ☐ Progress in years (more normal for those 65 or older)
- ☐ Hypertension (hypertension)
- ☐ High glucose (diabetes)
- ☐ Being overweight or corpulent
- ☐ Smoking
- ☐ Drinking a lot of liquor
- ☐ Being genuinely idle
- ☐ Being socially secluded
- ☐ Discouragement

Dementia is a condition that can be brought about by various illnesses that, over the long run, obliterate nerve cells and harm the mind, regularly prompting a weakening in mental capability (for example, the capacity to deal with thought) past what may be generally anticipated from the typical outcomes of organic maturing. While awareness isn't impacted, the weakness in mental capability is generally accompanied, and sometimes preceded, by changes in temperament, close to home control, conduct, or inspiration.

Dementia has physical, mental, social, and monetary effects for individuals living with dementia, as well as for their caregivers, families, and society overall. There is much of the time an absence of mindfulness and comprehension of dementia, bringing about derision and hindrances to finding and caring for it.

Normal types of dementia

Dementia is brought about by various infections or wounds that straightforwardly and by implication harm the mind. Alzheimer infection is the most well-known structure and may account for 60–70% of cases. Different structures incorporate vascular dementia, dementia with Lewy bodies (strange stories of protein inside nerve cells), and a gathering of infections that add to frontotemporal dementia (degeneration of the cerebrum of the mind).

Dementia may likewise foster after a stroke or with regards to specific contaminants like HIV because of unsafe utilization of liquor, dreary actual wounds to the cerebrum (known as ongoing horrendous encephalopathy), or nourishing inadequacies. The limits between various types of dementia are ill-defined, and blended frames frequently exist together.

Treatment and care

There is no solution for dementia, yet it should be possible to help the two individuals living with the sickness and the people who care for them.
Individuals with dementia can do whatever it takes to keep up with their personal satisfaction and advance their prosperity by:

Being actually dynamic partaking in exercises and social cooperation that animate the mind and keep up with everyday capability.

Likewise, a few prescriptions can assist with overseeing dementia side effects:

Cholinesterase inhibitors like donepezil are utilized to treat Alzheimer's disease. NMDA receptor bad guys like memantine are utilized for extreme Alzheimer's disease and vascular dementia. Medications to control circulatory strain and cholesterol can forestall extra harm to the cerebrum because of vascular dementia. Particular serotonin reuptake inhibitors (SSRIs) can assist with serious side effects of wretchedness in individuals living with dementia in the event that way of life and social changes don't work, yet these ought not be the main choice.

In the event that individuals living with dementia are in danger of harming themselves or others, drugs like haloperidol and risperidone can help; however, these ought to never be utilized as the principal treatment.

Taking care of oneself

There is no cure for dementia, but a lot can be done to support both people living with the illness and those who care for them.

For those determined to have dementia, there are things that can assist with overseeing side effects:

1. Remain genuinely dynamic
2. Eat soundly
3. Quit smoking and drinking liquor
4. Get ordinary check-ups with your primary care physician

5. Record ordinary assignments and arrangements to assist you with recalling significant things
6. Keep up your leisure activities and do things that you appreciate
7. Attempt better approaches to keep your psyche dynamic
8. Invest energy with loved ones and take part in local area life
9. Prepare for time

Over the long run, making significant choices for yourself or your finances might be more earnest;

1. Recognize individuals you trust to help you in deciding and assist you with imparting your decisions.
2. Make a development intent to let individuals know what your decisions and inclinations are for care and backing.
3. Carry your ID with your location and crisis contacts while going out.
4. Connect with loved ones for help.
5. Converse with individuals with whom you are familiar about the ways in which they can help you. Join a nearby care group. It is critical to perceive that giving consideration and backing to an individual living with dementia can be testing, influencing the caregiver's own wellbeing and prosperity.

As somebody supporting an individual living with dementia, contact relatives, companions, and experts for help. Enjoy ordinary reprieves and care for yourself. Attempt to pressure the executives with strategies, for example, care-based activities, and look for proficient assistance and direction if necessary.

Risk variables and anticipationIn spite of the fact that age is the most groundedly realized risk factor for dementia, it's anything but an unavoidable outcome of organic maturing. Further, dementia doesn't solely influence more seasoned individuals; youthful beginning dementia (characterized as the beginning of side effects before the age of 65 years) represents up to 9% of cases.

Concentrates demonstrate the way that individuals can diminish their risk of mental deterioration and dementia by being genuinely dynamic, not smoking, keeping away from destructive utilization of liquor, controlling their weight, eating a sound eating regimen, and keeping up with solid pulse, cholesterol, and glucose levels. Extra gamble factors incorporate despondency, social separation, low instructive fulfillment, mental dormancy, and air contamination.

Common libertiesTragically, individuals living with dementia are regularly denied the essential privileges and opportunities accessible to other people. In numerous nations, physical and substance restrictions are widely utilized in care homes for more established individuals and in intense consideration settings, in any event, when guidelines are set up to maintain the privileges of individuals to opportunity and decision.

A proper and strong authoritative climate in light of universally acknowledged basic freedom principles is expected to guarantee the greatest level of care for individuals with dementia and their caregivers.

WHO reaction

WHO perceives dementia as a general well being need. In May 2017, the World Wellbeing Gathering embraced the worldwide activity to anticipate the general wellbeing reaction to dementia in 2017–2025. The Arrangement gives an exhaustive plan to activity for strategy creators worldwide, local and public accomplices, and WHO in the accompanying regions: tending to dementia as a general well being need; expanding familiarity with dementia and making a dementia-comprehensive society; lessening the gamble of dementia; finding, treatment, and care; data frameworks for dementia; support for dementia caregivers; and also examination and development.

To work with the checking of the worldwide dementia activity plan, WHO fostered the Worldwide Dementia Observatory (GDO), an information entryway that gathers country information on 35 key dementia markers across the worldwide activity plan's seven vital regions. As a supplement to the GDO, WHO sent off the GDO Information Trade Stage, which is a storehouse of good practice models in the space of dementia, fully intent on encouraging common learning and multi-directional trade between locales, nations, and people worldwide.

Different Types of Dementia

Alzheimer's disease
Vascular dementia
Lewy body disease
Frontotemporal dementia
Alcohol-related dementia
Human immunodeficiency virus-associated dementia
Younger-onset dementia
Dementia caused by Huntington's disease
Creutzfeldt-Jakob disease

Dementia is an expansive term used to portray the side effects of a huge gathering of diseases that influence the cerebrum and cause an ever-evolving decrease in an individual's work. It isn't an explicit infection. Dementia side effects incorporate cognitive decline, disarray, and character and social changes. These side effects disrupt the individual's social and working lives.

Dementia is more common in individuals north of 65, yet it's anything but a typical piece of maturing. Various diseases can bring about dementia, and each has its own elements. Much of the time, the reason individuals foster these circumstances isn't known.

☐ Alzheimer's disease

Alzheimer's disease is the most widely recognized type of dementia and accounts for roughly 66% of cases. A dynamic degenerative sickness goes after the mind and causes slow expansion in mental (memory and thinking) issues.

In Alzheimer's disease, the actual harm to the cerebrum is brought about by amyloid plaques and neurofibrillary tangles. The plaques (stringy patches) structure when a protein called beta-amyloid structures strange bunches. The knots are contorted strands of a protein called tau.

The majority of the instances of Alzheimer's infection are not caused by known changes in explicit qualities. This type is called irregular Alzheimer's illness and, for the most part, happens in individuals over 65 years old. Familial Alzheimer's illness is an uncommon kind that is acquired, with side effects frequently appearing when the individual is somewhere in the range of 40 and 60. In familial Alzheimer's illness, hereditary changes in three explicit qualities cause an expansion in the development of the protein present in amyloid plaques.

Practically all individuals with Down disorder will get Alzheimer's infection, and it will happen at a younger age than those without the condition. Individuals with Down syndrome produce a greater amount of the protein that structures amyloid plaques in Alzheimer's disease. This is on the grounds that they have an additional duplicate of chromosome 21 that contains the quality that produces amyloid protein.

☐ Vascular dementia

Vascular dementia is an expansive term for dementia related to sickness in the veins of the mind. This vein illness influences the dissemination of blood to the mind and causes harm.

Vascular dementia might seem like Alzheimer's disease. A combination of Alzheimer's disease and vascular dementia can happen in certain individuals. Vascular dementia is the second most common type of dementia, and there are various sorts.

Key infarct dementia
A solitary, huge stroke can at times cause vital infarct dementia, contingent upon the size and area of the stroke. An enormous stroke can bring about unexpected beginnings of side effects, including conduct or thinking. The sort of side effects will depend on the region of the mind that was harmed by the stroke.

Assuming no further strokes happen, once in a while, the side effects of dementia can balance out or try to get better after some time. Assuming there is other sickness in the veins of the cerebrum or, again, on the off chance that the individual has another stroke, the side effects of dementia might deteriorate.

Multi-infarct dementia
This sort of vascular dementia is brought about by various little strokes, called smaller than normal strokes or transient ischaemic assaults (TIAs). This is brought about by sickness in the enormous veins of the cerebrum. The strokes are frequently 'quiet', implying that the individual doesn't realize that they are having little strokes.

As additional strokes happen, the harm in the cerebrum increases, and thinking and its abilities are impacted. Discouragement and emotional episodes can happen; however, the side effects depend on the area of the stroke.

Multi-infarct dementia can have a stepwise movement, where side effects demolish after another stroke, then balance out for a period.

Subcortical vascular dementia
Otherwise called Binswanger's illness, this sort of vascular dementia is brought about by sickness in the

little veins profound inside the mind, which harms the subcortical (profound) region of the cerebrum. Subcortical vascular dementia can be connected with untreated hypertension or diabetes that prompts vascular illness. It is brought about by hypertension, thickening of the corridors, and a deficient blood stream.

Side effects frequently incorporate weakening of thinking and thinking abilities, gentle memory issues, strolling and development issues, social changes, and an absence of bladder control.
Subcortical vascular dementia is normally moderate, with side effects deteriorating over the long haul as more vascular harm happens, although the individual's capacities can vary.

☐ Lewy body infection

Lewy body sickness (LBD) is an umbrella term that depicts conditions portrayed by the arrangement of bunches in the mind called Lewy bodies. Clusters develop in synapses and are made of a protein called alpha-synuclein. These bunches happen in an unambiguous region of the mind, causing changes in development, thinking, and conduct.
Individuals with LBD might encounter enormous changes in consideration and thinking. They can go from practically ordinary execution to extreme disarray within brief periods. Visual mental trips are likewise a typical side effect.

LBD is known as a range of illnesses since three covering conditions fall under the umbrella term, including:
dementia with lewy bodiesParkinson's illnessParkinson's illness and dementiaThese circumstances include the arrangement of Lewy bodies; however, the planning of the side effects will decide the conclusion.

LBD sometimes happens alongside Alzheimer's disease and vascular dementia. The covering of side effects can make the determination of LBD troublesome, with the exception of Parkinson's sickness, which has laid out techniques for conclusion. This means that on the off chance that the development's side effects show up first, the conclusion is more clear than if the side effects of dementia show up first.

Dementia with Lewy bodiesIn the event that the principal side effects seem to be changes to the individual's reasoning and conduct, the analysis will be dementia with Lewy bodies.

Parkinson's illness
On the off chance that the primary side effects seem to be development side effects, the determination will be Parkinson's illness. These side effects include earthquakes, firmness in appendages and joints, discourse hindrances, and trouble starting actual developments.

Parkinson's disease, dementiaThe vast majority of people with Parkinson's illness will develop side effects of dementia. In the event that the side effects influencing development show up first and are followed by side effects influencing thinking and conduct, the determination will be Parkinson's disease or dementia. Frontotemporal dementiaFrontotemporal dementia (FTD) is the name given to a gathering of dementias that include degeneration in either of the front-facing or transient curves of the cerebrum. It is now and then called frontotemporal lobar degeneration, or Pick's infection.

The front-facing and worldly curves of the mind are associated with temperament, social ways of behaving, consideration, judgment, arranging, and poise. Harm to these regions of the mind can prompt a diminishing in scholarly capacities and changes in character, feeling, and conduct. Harm can likewise cause trouble perceiving articles or understanding or communicating language.

Not at all like Alzheimer's illness, memory probably won't be impacted, particularly in the beginning phases. The side effects will depend on what portion of the mind is harmed. At the point when the cerebrums are impacted first, the fundamental changes are in character and conduct, though harm to the worldly curves influences language abilities.

FTD regularly influences individuals at a younger age than Alzheimer's disease, with side effects starting between the ages of 50 and 70 and becoming more youthful once in a while.

Conduct variation FTDIn the front-facing or conduct variation of FTD, there are changes in the individual's way of behaving, propensities, character, or profound reactions. Side effects change from one individual to another, contingent upon which region of the cerebrum is harmed. Certain individuals with conduct variation FTD become exceptionally emotionless, while others will lose their hindrances.

Semantic dementia
In the worldly curve type of FTD, the underlying side effect is typically a decrease in language capacity. In semantic dementia, the capacity to assign significance to words is continuously lost. Perusing, spelling, perception, and articulation are typically impacted.

Moderate non-familiar aphasia
Moderate non-familiar aphasia (PNFA) is the most unusual type of FTD and will, in general, have a later beginning. The capacity to talk easily is slowly being lost. Individuals with PNFA experience issues imparting because of the slow and troublesome creation of words, the contortion of discourse, and an inclination to deliver some unacceptable words.
Acquired FTDA few types of FTD are acquired and are brought about by unambiguous hereditary changes.

Familial FTD represents something like 10 to 15 percent of all FTD cases. Two qualities represent around 50% of familial FTD cases: the tau protein and the progranulin protein. A few other more uncommon hereditary changes cause FTD. For impacted families, hereditary testing is accessible.

- Frontotemporal dementia with Parkinsonism 17 (FTDP-17)One type of familial FTD, otherwise called frontotemporal dementia with Parkinsonism-17 (FTDP-17), is brought about by hereditary changes in the quality of tau protein, situated on chromosome 17. No other risk factors for this condition are known.

FTDP-17 is interesting and represents just three percent of all instances of dementia. Side effects dynamically deteriorate after some time and, as a rule, show up between the ages of 40 and 60. The condition influences both reasoning and social abilities, as well as developments like inflexibility, absence of look, and issues with balance (like Parkinson's infection).

It may very well be troubling to be informed that you (or a relative) have a hereditary problem or are in danger of having one. Hereditary directing furnishes the individual and their family with data about a hereditary problem and its probable influence on their lives. This can help an individual with FTDP-17 come to informed clinical and individual conclusions about how to deal with their condition and the difficulties it presents to their (and their family's) wellbeing and prosperity. Pre-birth hereditary guidance is likewise accessible for guardians to assist them with making a choice about a pregnancy that might be in danger of FTDP-17.

☐ Alcohol-related dementia

An excess of liquor, especially whenever related to an eating regimen lacking in thiamine (vitamin B1), can prompt irreversible cerebrum harm. Many specialists lean toward the terms 'liquor-related cerebrum injury' or 'liquor-related mind hindrance', as opposed to liquor-related dementia, since liquor misuse can cause impedances in various mental capabilities.

The weakest pieces of the mind are those utilized for memory, arranging, coordinating, and judgment; interactive abilities; and equilibrium.
This sort of dementia is preventable. The Public Wellbeing and Clinical Exploration Gathering of Australia suggests that people drink something like two standard beverages each day to decrease the risk of medical conditions related to liquor.

Wernicke-Korsakoff disorder is in some cases alluded to as alcoholic dementia or liquor-related dementia; however, it is brought about by thiamine deficiency as opposed to being an immediate consequence of liquor misuse.

Wernicke's encephalopathyLiquor harms the coating of the stomach and influences the assimilation of nutrients. The subsequent absence of thiamine can cause Wernicke's encephalopathy.
Side effects of this condition include:
jerky eye developments, loss of motion of muscles moving the eyes, or twofold vision loss of muscle coordination, unfortunate equilibrium, faltering, or a failure to walk disarray.High portions of thiamine can be utilized to treat the condition, and most side effects ought to be switched.

Assuming left untreated, long-lasting cerebrum harm and demise can happen.
Korsakoff's conditionWernicke's encephalopathy that is untreated or not treated soon enough can prompt Korsakoff's condition. Korsakoff's disorder can likewise create all-around It typically grows steadily, and the harm is mostly to the region of the cerebrum that is significant for momentary memory.

Side effects of Korsakoff's condition include:

Present moment (and now and again, long haul) cognitive decline failure to frame new recollections or learn new data character changes making up stories to fill holes in memory (confabulation)seeing or hearing things that aren't actually there (pipedreams)absence of knowledge about the condition.The advancement of Korsakoff's disorder can be halted on the off chance that the individual totally goes without liquor, embraces a sound eating regimen, and takes nutrient enhancements. Thiamine supplementation might assist in preventing further mental harm from happening.

- ☐ Human immunodeficiency infection-related dementia

Human immunodeficiency infection (HIV)-related dementia (HAD) is an inconvenience that influences certain individuals with HIV and AIDS (Helps). This condition was known as Helps-related dementia or Helps dementia complex (ADC).
HAD is related to serious mental, engine, and conduct issues that hinder everyday working and diminish freedom and personal satisfaction. It is exceptional in individuals in the early phases of HIV/AIDS, yet may increase as the illness progresses.

Not every person who has HIV/AIDS will develop HAD. It is remembered to influence around seven percent of individuals with HIV/AIDS who are not taking anti-HIV drugs.

HAD is the most extreme type of HIV-related neurocognitive confusion (HAND). Milder structures influence mental capabilities (thinking abilities like memory, language, consideration, and arranging), but not to the degree that a determination of dementia is justified.

In Australia, where the vast majority of people who are HIV-positive get treatment with mixed antiretroviral treatment, HAD is luckily extraordinary. Nonetheless, notwithstanding powerful treatment, the milder types of HAD influence numerous HIV-positive individuals.

☐ Youger onset dementia

The term more youthful beginning dementia is generally used to describe any type of dementia analyzed in individuals younger than 65 years. It is likewise sometimes called beginning-stage dementia.

Dementia in more youthful individuals is significantly less normal than dementia happening after the age of 65; however, it is now and again analyzed in individuals between the ages of 30 and 60. More youthful beginnings: dementia can be challenging to analyze, and it isn't clear how inescapable it is. Specific types of dementia are more probable in more youthful individuals, including familial Alzheimer's disease and frontotemporal dementia.

☐ Dementia brought about by Huntington's illness

Huntington's syndrome is an acquired degenerative cerebrum infection that influences the psyche and body.

It typically shows up between the ages of 30 and 50 and is characterized by scholarly decay and unpredictable compulsory development of the appendages or facial muscles. Different side effects incorporate character change, memory aggravation, slurred discourse, hindered judgment, and mental issues.

There is no treatment accessible to stop the movement of this illness, yet drugs have some control over development problems and mental side effects. Dementia happens in most individuals with Huntington's disease.

☐ Creutzfeldt-Jakob sickness

Creutzfeldt-Jakob sickness (CJD) is a very intriguing and deadly mind problem brought about by a protein molecule called a prion. It happens to one in every million individuals. The two sorts of CJD are: Exemplary CJD incorporates inconsistent and familial (exceptionally uncommon) structures.variation CJD connected with 'frantic cow sickness'.Early side effects incorporate dementia, bombing memory, changes of conduct, and an absence of coordination. As the sickness advances for the most part quickly mental disintegration becomes articulated, compulsory developments show up, and the individual might become visually impaired, foster shortcoming in the arms or legs, and, at last, pass into a state of unconsciousness.

Common Symptoms and Progression

Dementia is an umbrella term for a range of moderate problems influencing the cerebrum.
There are more than 200 types of dementia. Alzheimer's disease is the most well-known. Each kind of dementia stops an individual's synapses from working in unambiguous regions, influencing their memorable capacity to think and talk.
Specialists normally utilize the word 'dementia' to portray a bunch of normal side effects that deteriorate over the long haul, especially:

- Memory issues
- Expanding carelessness
- Trouble holding new data
- Losing all sense of direction in places that used to be recognizable
- Battling with names
- Losing things as often as possible
- Mental capacity
- Trouble grasping the overall setting, e.g., getting up around midnight to go to work, regardless of whether they're resigned
- Trouble with picking what to purchase and paying while shopping
- Battling with direction and thinking
- Loss of interest in exercises they used to appreciate

- Fretfulness, e.g., pacing, squirming, and attempting to take off from the house
- Correspondence
- Battling to track down the right words
- Rehashing the same thing frequently
- Trouble making and following discussion
- Trouble perusing and composing
- Becoming calmer and more removed
- Loss of interest in mingling
- Loss of certainty
- Changes in character and conduct
- State of mind swings, tension, and melancholy

In spite of the fact that dementia has a typical arrangement of side effects, each type introduces itself in an unexpected way, and individuals might have some of the side effects in general. They may likewise have more than one sort of dementia ('blended dementia'), with side effects of each.

Signs and side effects

Changes in state of mind and conduct now and again happen even before memory issues happen. Side effects deteriorate over the long run. At last, a great many people with dementia will require others to assist with day-to-day exercises.

Early signs and side effects are:

Failing to remember things or ongoing occasions

Losing or losing things

Getting lost while strolling or driving

Being befuddled, even in recognizable spots

Forgetting about time

Hardships tackling issues or deciding issues

Following discussions or inconvenience tracking down words hardships

Performing recognizable assignments

Misconceiving distances to objects outwardly.

Normal changes in state of mind and conduct include:

feeling restless, miserable, or furious about cognitive decline

character changes

unseemly way of behaving

withdrawal from work or social exercises

being less inspired by others' feelings.

Dementia influences every individual in a different way, contingent on the fundamental causes, other ailments, and the individual's mental workings prior to turning out to be sick.

Most side effects become more awful over the long haul, while others could vanish or just happen in the later phases of dementia. As the infection advances, the requirement for individual consideration increases. Individuals with dementia will most likely be unable to perceive relatives or companions, foster challenges moving around, let completely go of their bladders and bowls, experience difficulty eating and drinking, and experience conduct changes, for example, hostility that are troubling to the individual with dementia as well as everyone around them.

Influence on the Individual and Guardian
In 2017, the Alzheimer's Association finished a broad study on the impacts of Alzheimer's on the family guardian. Years later, investigations of Alzheimer's and dementia have observed that the impacts of these illnesses on the family's parental figures are more central than at any time in recent memory.

As a matter of fact, their continuous examination of Alzheimer's disease and different types of dementia keeps on demonstrating an impractical physical, monetary, and profound weight on parental figures.

Dementia influences the guardian and their loved ones. Really focusing on a friend or family member with moderate cognitive decline can influence typical everyday life in different ways. Parental figures report a more noteworthy number of physical and profound medical issues and, generally speaking, worse health compared to non-guardians. Levels of mental misery are essentially higher in dementia parental figures than in different sorts of care. Also, guardians will quite often forfeit their own relaxation interests and leisure activities, lessen time with loved ones, and surrender or decrease work to dedicate time to their adored one.

Dementia influences family finances. The Alzheimer's Affiliation 2017 Alzheimer's Sickness Raw Numbers report shows that individuals age 65 and older seasoned with Alzheimer's or dementia endure a normal of 4 to 10 years after conclusion, for certain living up to 20 years. Families ordinarily step in as the parental figure, particularly from the get-go in the analysis. This can affect the family guardian, particularly assuming the consideration was impromptu. Much of the time, the relative aides pay for the personal expenses related to dementia care, and that implies they frequently cut back on their own spending to do so. Furthermore, some likewise decrease their work hours or even quit their paying responsibilities to become full-time family parents.

Character changes can cause significant damage. Character changes in a friend or family member with dementia are, in many cases, the most troublesome aspect of the illness for family guardians to make due. Once in a while, an individual impacted by dementia might become forceful on the grounds that they don't have any idea of what other means to put themselves out there. Others might encounter tension, unsettledness, or touchiness. Disarray likewise seems while attempting to follow through with the everyday responsibilities the vast majority of us underestimate. Tragically, these character changes can likewise negatively affect the family parental figure and, at times, adversely influence their wellbeing.

Numerous family guardians who care for friends and family living with Alzheimer's and dementia handle the consideration all alone. In any case, recruiting a guardian to help with the everyday can offer truly necessary rest and genuine serenity to the family parental figure and help the individual impacted by the illness to carry on with their other lives with reason.

Impact on the Individual and Caregiver

In 2017, the Alzheimer's Association finished a broad review of the impacts of Alzheimer's on the family's parental figures. Years later, investigations of Alzheimer's and dementia have observed that the impacts of these illnesses on the family guardian are more vital than at any other time in recent memory.

As a matter of fact, their continuous exploration of Alzheimer's disease and different types of dementia keeps on demonstrating an impractical physical, monetary, and profound weight on guardians.

Dementia influences the guardian and their loved ones. Really focusing on a friend or family member with moderate cognitive decline can influence typical day-to-day life in different ways. Guardians report a more noteworthy number of physical and profound medical conditions and more awful overall well being compared to non-parental figures. Levels of mental trouble are altogether higher in dementia parental figures than in different sorts of care. What's more, parental figures will quite often forfeit their own recreation interests and leisure activities, decrease time with loved ones, and surrender or diminish work to give time to their adored one.

Dementia influences family finances. The Alzheimer's Affiliation 2017 Alzheimer's Sickness Statistical Data

Points Report demonstrates that individuals aged 65 and older seasoned with Alzheimer's or dementia endure a normal of 4 to 10 years after finding, for certain living up to 20 years. Families commonly step in as the parental figure, particularly from the get-go in the analysis. This can affect the family guardian, particularly in the event that the consideration was spontaneous. As a rule, the relative aides pay for the personal expenses related to dementia care, and that implies they frequently cut back on their own spending to do so. What's more, some likewise decrease their work hours or even quit their paying tasks to become full-time family guardians.

Character changes can cause significant damage. Character changes in a friend or family member with dementia are, in many cases, the most troublesome aspect of the illness for family guardians to make due. In some cases, an individual impacted by dementia might become forceful on the grounds that they don't have the foggiest idea of what other means to communicate their thoughts. Others might encounter uneasiness, tumult, or touchiness.

Disarray likewise seems to occur while attempting to finish the everyday jobs that a large portion of us underestimate. Tragically, these character changes can likewise negatively affect the family parental figure and, now and again, adversely influence their wellbeing.

Numerous family guardians who care for friends and family living with Alzheimer's and dementia handle the consideration all alone. However, recruiting a parental figure to help with the everyday can offer truly necessary reprieve and an inward feeling of harmony to the family guardian and help the individual impacted by the illness carry on with their other lives with reason.

Chapter three

Dementia Behaviors: A Comprehensive Understanding

Agitation and Restlessness:

Agitation is a critical issue for the elderly, their families, and their guardians. Although a significant part of the writing on disturbance is pharmacologic in nature, a few papers exhibit segmented and ecological ways to deal with the issue. The writing audit highlights the holes in both the appraisal and the information on the peculiarity. A calculated system and a thorough philosophy should be produced for concentrating on disturbance. On these bases, exploration could investigate the signs of tumult and the recurrence of events, inclining factors for fomentation, encouraging elements that trigger disturbance, the results of unsettling for the older and for their overseers, and the viability of elective mediations.

Fretfulness, including squirming, pacing, and attempting to leave the home, is normal in individuals with dementia.
It tends to be disturbing for the individual, particularly assuming they are kept from moving around, and for relatives, who may specifically stress over the individual's security.

Anxiety and Fear

It is normal for individuals with dementia to have uneasiness. It can exacerbate side effects, especially those that influence an individual's consideration, arranging, putting together, and navigation.

Individuals who have had uneasiness in the past are bound to have it once more. Anyway, individuals in the beginning phases of dementia might have uneasiness that is connected straightforwardly to their stresses over their memory and what's to come.

Individuals with vascular dementia frequently have a better understanding and consciousness of their condition than individuals with Alzheimer's illness. This might make sense of why it's more normal for individuals with vascular dementia to have tension.

Individuals who live in a considered home might have nervousness that is connected to an absence of individual consideration and necessities that are neglected. For instance, they might have nobody to converse with routinely or do daytime exercises to keep them dynamic. As their condition advances, individuals with dementia become more disoriented, neglectful, and less ready to thoroughly consider things. For certain individuals, this battle to figure out the world can cause uneasiness.

Repeating and Disorientation:

Getting lost while driving or strolling in natural regions and not having the option to review the date, day of the week, or time might be early indications of dementia. Confounding constantly (say by resting during the day and remaining conscious the greater part of the evening), not knowing the season or year, and preparing for a get-together or arrangement on some unacceptable day indicate time bewilderment.

Somebody who gets derailed or confounded in their own home (maybe they begin searching for the refrigerator or pot in the room or restroom), experiences issues in recollecting how to get to a companion's home, or who battles to find their strategy for getting around recognizable shops, workplaces, or different structures is giving indications of spot confusion.

Sundowning and Sleep Disturbances:

Numerous more established adults have issues resting, yet individuals with dementia frequently have a considerably harder time. Rest aggravation might influence up to 25% of individuals with mild to direct dementia and half of individuals with extreme dementia. Rest aggravations will quite often deteriorate as dementia advances in seriousness.

Conceivable rest issues incorporate exorbitant tiredness during the day and a sleeping disorder with trouble nodding off and staying unconscious. Regular enlightenments during the evening and untimely morning arousals are likewise normal.

Individuals with dementia could likewise encounter a peculiarity at night or during the night called sundowning. They could feel befuddled, upset, restless, and forceful. Late-night meandering from this perspective can be dangerous.

Obstructive rest apnea is likewise more common in individuals with Alzheimer's disease. This possibly serious rest problem makes breathing over and again pause and begin during rest.

Factors that could add to unsettling influences and sundowning include:

- Mental and actual weariness by the day's end
- Changes in the body clock
- A requirement for less rest, which is normal among more established adults
- Confusion

- Decreased lighting and expanded shadows, which can make individuals with dementia become befuddled and apprehensive.

At the point when a friend or family member wakes during the evening assuming the individual with dementia wakes during the evening, remain mentally collected despite the fact that you may be depleted yourself. Try not to contend. All things considered, ask what the individual requirements are. Evening tumult may be brought about by distress or torment.

Check whether you can decide the wellspring of the issue, like obstruction, a full bladder, or a room that is excessively hot or cold.

Delicately remind the person in question that it's evening and time for rest. Assuming that the individual needs to pace, don't control the person in question. All things considered, permit it under your watch.

Wandering and Safety Concerns

Wandering is a typical behavior in patients with Alzheimer's disease or different types of dementia. What's more, when the singular starts to give indications of wandering ways of behaving, they are at a high risk of going astray or getting derailed.

This conduct can be extremely upsetting for guardians and perilous for the person.

There are steps that guardians can take to assist with forestalling meandering or make it hard for the individual to go astray and incorporate such things as:

Establishing a protected climate by…

1. Locks on entryways
2. Entryway or window cautions
3. Getting vehicle keys
4. Kid verification door handle covers
5. Not letting the individual be at home or in a vehicle
6. Get an area GPS beacon for the individual.

Overseeing fretful ways of behaving with…

- Exercises to involve the individual's time
- Ordinary, actual activity
- Guaranteeing sufficient rest
- Announcing conduct changes or expanded disarray to the individual's primary care physician

What to Do If Your Cherished One Goes Astray:

There's no time to waste. It is critical to not defer activity. A few quick advances you can take are:

- Inform the police right away. Call 911.
- Have a wellness plan set up and a telephone tree to caution loved ones.
- Prepare nearby organizations and neighbors before an event of meandering to build familiarity with your friends and family's conditions and propensities.
- Utilize online entertainment when applicable. A few states have Silver Cautions. In Pennsylvania, the state police regulate the Absent and Imperiled Individual Warning Framework.

Contact your nearby state police sleeping enclosure as quickly as time permits.

Aggression and Irritability

A forceful way of behaving might be:
verbal: for instance, swearing, shouting, yelling, or conveying intimidation
physical for instance, hitting, squeezing, scratching, hair-pulling, gnawing, or tossing things.

Certain individuals expect that a forceful way of behaving is a side effect of dementia itself. This can be valid; however, almost certainly, there is another reason. It's critical to see past the way people behave and

ponder what might be causing it. Purposes behind the individual's way of behaving could include:
Hardships to do with dementia for instance, cognitive decline, language or direction issues.

Their psychological and actual wellbeing for instance, they might have agony or distress that they can't impartThe amount and kind of contact they have with someone else or others.

Their actual environmental elements for instance, assuming the room is too dull, the individual might become confused and upset since they can't resolve where they are feeling of being crazy, disappointment with the manner in which others are acting, or an inclination that they're not being paid attention to or perceived.

Dissatisfaction and disarray at not having the option to get things done or at not having the option to figure out what's going on around them.

Hallucinations and Delusions

Dementia influences individuals in various ways, and changes in the way of behaving or the profound condition of somebody living with dementia are normal.

Individuals living with dementia, in some cases, experience bogus discernments or thoughts. Despite the fact that pipedreams and fancies are nonexistent, they appear to be genuine to the individual encountering them. They can cause outrageous tension and frenzy.

Hallucinations: Pipedreams are tangible encounters that can't be checked by any other person. Normally, somebody sees something not there (like an individual) or hears something others can't hear (like voices or startling sounds). Be that as it may, mind flights can incorporate any of the faculties.

Delusions: Hallucinations are unequivocally held thoughts that are not in view of the real world or realities but rather are believed to be valid. The individual might have daydreams about others taking their cash or assets. Or, on the other hand, they might have fixed thoughts regarding individuals proposing to hurt them.

Chapter Four

Compassionate Love and the Dementia Caregiver

Empathetic love is "a disposition toward others, either close others or outsiders or all of humankind; containing feelings, perceptions, and ways of behaving that are centered around caring concern, delicacy, and a direction toward supporting, helping, and figuring out the others. especially when the others are seen to be enduring or out of luck.

Cultivating Empathy and Understanding

Sympathy is an ideal capacity for one to stroll from another person's point of view. To encounter their reality to acquire a more profound comprehension of what he or she is encountering. For those in dementia care, venturing into their reality is frequently particularly testing, as ways of behaving and feelings can change quickly and suddenly.

The "AHA" second is enormous when a considerate accomplice can feel the dissatisfaction, uneasiness, dread, weakness, and loneliness that living with dementia frequently sustains. This opens a considerate accomplice's eyes, subsequently moving them to draw on this intrinsic feeling of compassion.

Nurturing Emotional Connection

Dementia can cause changes in the way people behave toward their companions, friends, and family. Such changes are extremely normal, yet they can put tremendous weight on families and caregivers. It very well may be disturbing when somebody who has recently been delicate and cherishing acts in a peculiar or forceful manner.

Adapting to new ways of behaving can be extremely challenging and is often a question of experimentation. Continuously recall that the way of behaving is brought about by the condition.

Recognizing Personal Histories and Memories

In the previous stages, cognitive decline and disarray might have been gentle. The individual with dementia might know about and be disappointed by the progressions occurring, for example, trouble reviewing ongoing occasions or deciding or handling information disclosed by others.

In the later stages, cognitive decline becomes undeniably more extreme. An individual may not perceive relatives, may fail to remember connections, call relatives by different names, or become confounded about the area of home or the progression of time. The individual might fail to remember the motivation behind normal things, like a pen or a fork. These progressions are probably the absolute most excruciating for guardians and families.

Promoting Dignity and Autonomy

Worry for the independence of an individual with dementia requires an evaluation of the individual's skill or ability to figure out the important choices.Furthermore, the results of a specific errand or choice considering one's own qualities Decisions about capability in a particular region are regularly made casually by going to doctors, other medical services experts, and relatives. Such appraisals can be straightforward and in light of presence of mind, especially when the individual is clearly muddled in discussion, holds practically no data, answers similar rehashed questions with contradicting proclamations, and needs knowledge of the outcomes of a choice or its other options. In the event that data is neither handled nor controlled, an evaluation is easy. Be that as it may, an appraisal of capability may not be conclusive on the grounds that an individual might be clearly uncouth one day yet skilled the following. Indeed, even the individual with to some degree progressed dementia might have times of clarity.that take into account huge directions.

Self-Care for the Caregiver

Dealing with yourself genuinely and intellectually is perhaps one of the main things you can do as a Caregiver. This could mean asking relatives and companions to assist, doing things you appreciate, or finding support from a home medical care administration. Making these moves can bring you some relief. Additionally, it may assist in holding you back from getting sick or discouraged. A man sitting with his back to the camera at the oceanside.

Ways of dealing with yourself…

Here are a few different ways you can deal with yourself:
- Request help when you want it.
- Eat good food varieties.
- Join a caregivers group.
- Enjoy reprieves every day.
- Invest energy in companions.
- Stay aware of your leisure activities and interests.
- Practice as frequently as possible.
- See your PCP consistently.
- Keep your wellbeing, lawfulness, and monetary data forward-thinking.

55

Chapter five

Effective Communication Strategies

Non-Verbal Communication Techniques

Non-verbal communication is conveying without the utilization of expressed words. You could utilize motions, looks, and non-verbal communication to speak with the individual you care for. These may turn out to be a portion of the principal ways an individual with dementia communicates as their condition advances.

Active Listening and Validation

Active Listening and Validation: utilizing eye-to-eye connection to take a gander at the individual and empowering them to take a gander at you when both of you are talking. making an effort not to hinder them, regardless of whether you assume you understand what they're talking about.

That is the reason approval treatment, or the approval strategy is a particularly valuable approach to moving toward individuals with dementia. In the briefest terms, it is an approach to sympathetically entering the universe of somebody who has dementia. Rather than battling with them to acknowledge your situation, you work on entering theirs.

Using Visual Aids and Simple Instructions:

Various visual guides, signs, and pictures can assist somebody with tracking down things or rooms in the home or briefing them about occasions or arrangements. Sights, sounds, surfaces, scents, and tastes permit somebody living with dementia to encounter the world at their own speed through their faculties.

Utilize basic words and sentences. Talk gradually, unmistakably, and in a consoling tone. Abstain from raising your voice higher or stronger; all things considered, pitch your voice lower. In the event that she doesn't grasp the initial time, utilize similar phrasing to rehash your message or question.

Reducing Distractions for Better communication:

Dementia is a dynamic problem with numerous side effects, including conduct issues. Thus, it's normal for more seasoned adults to end up being confused, irate, unsettled, and, surprisingly, brutal. Family guardians need to foster interruption strategies like those referenced below, which can quiet circumstances and redirect their old adored one's consideration.

1. Play music.Music memory is one of the capabilities that typically stay with more established adults living with dementia. Regardless of whether your adored one neglects individuals' names or faces, the person might recollect the words and hints of their main tunes. Playing these tunes could give a moment's interruption that helps your loved one's temperament and permits the person in question to zero in on certain things. Music can be an interruption procedure in all phases of dementia, which makes it considerably more valuable.

Side effects like fomentation, disarray, outrage, and disappointment are normal in older individuals with dementia. Dementia can be trying for seniors to make ends meet, yet they can keep a greater sense of existence with the assistance of expert dementia care. Barrie seniors can benefit incredibly from the Mental Therapeutics Strategy (CTM), an exercise-based program intended to advance mental wellbeing and defer the beginning of dementia. CTM is incorporated at no extra charge for any of the in-home consideration plans given by Home Consideration Help.

2. Attempt a fragrance-based treatment.Lighting candles or utilizing smell splashes can activate receptors in the mind that are answerable for the guideline of feelings. The aromas can keep side effects free from uneasiness and lower the risk of melancholy. At the point when you notice your cherished one becoming upset and bothered, light a candle, utilize a scented splash, or put

a couple of drops of natural ointment in a diffuser to occupy that person and strain in the room.

3. Begin another action. Fatigue and the powerlessness to stay aware of a discussion or a particular errand could cause confrontational conduct in more established adults with dementia. You can promptly redirect your loved one's consideration by beginning a new, less testing action. For instance, in the event that your folks are playing a card game and become exhausted and vexed, stop the game and have a go at something tomfoolery and more reasonable, like shading or moving. Your loved one can zero in on the new undertaking as opposed to pondering the difficulties related to the game.

Chapter six

Creating a Nurturing Environment:

As the essential parental figure of a friend or family member with dementia, you're mindful of the physical and inner difficulties they face consistently. You must ensure they're protected and agreeable in their home climate, and it's a difficult task.
You could feel that any home climate is okay for an individual with dementia all things considered, it's their own home, correct? Sadly, besides the fact that their recognizable environmental elements can mistake somebody for dementia, certain normal highlights of many homes can present potential dangers.

A home climate can encourage an individual residing with dementia to keep up with their capacities and give significant commitment by providing fundamental prompts and openness. It will urge a dementia patient to live as full and free a daily existence as could be expected.

Simplifying numerous alterations to their home, private mature care office, medical clinic, public structure, or arrangement, also known as compositional plan changes, can assist with working on the personal satisfaction of individuals with dementia.

Creating changes to the actual climate can help individuals with dementia feel more positive about their environmental factors, which can lessen disarray and nervousness.

That is why understanding how to establish a sympathetic and secure home climate for those with dementia is so significant.

Designing a Safe and Stimulating Living:

☐ Indoor regions

A mitigating, quiet climate is useful for everyone. For an individual with dementia, it can limit disarray and assist them with concentrating and resting. In a perfect world, the climate ought to likewise bring back cheerful memories.

Consider the family standard, the commotion levels, the lighting, the impacts of mirrors, the condition of the room, and, surprisingly, the varieties and examples utilized all through the house.

Many individuals with dementia find commotion irritating, so you could have to switch the TV and radio off more regularly. Attempt to wipe out shadows, brightness, and reflections that an individual with dementia might see as startling.

Some security tips to consider include:
ensuring the floors are not elusive, keeping away from free covers and other excursion dangers, and not having

an excess of messiness. A sufficiently bright house will likewise diminish the risk of falling.actually taking a look at the wellbeing of locks, floors, entryways, windows, steps, verandahs, and galleries to check whether they need changing.contemplating warming, cooling, lighting, power, and gas would they say they are protected and simple to utilize?Putting signs on taps to show which is hot and which is cold introducing sensor lights or lights with worked-in clocks, assuming the individual meanders around evening time.introducing handrails on the two sides of stepschecking glass entryways and windows with covering tapeIt is likewise vital to keep the home at an agreeable temperature on the grounds that the individual with dementia probably won't have the option to pass judgment on the actual temperature or recall how to change their garments assuming they are excessively hot or excessively cold.

☐ Outside regions

Outside regions ought to likewise be quiet, unwinding, and ok for an individual with dementia to stroll around in. For instance, you could place them in a raised nursery bed, which they could plant out and tend to. Put clocks on hoses to water the nursery without the individual expecting to make sure to switch the tap off when they are done.
Pets are a significant wellspring of solace and friendship for some individuals with dementia, yet it is vital to

guarantee the creature is being really focused on appropriately and can't get away.

You might have to fix and lock entryways. You might try and have to set up walls, despite the fact that you should do this cautiously since another wall can cause an individual with dementia to feel caught.
Consider eliminating deterrents from ways, concealing trash or fertilizer canisters, eliminating noxious or spiky plants, and locking away any perilous synthetic substances in the nursery shed or carport, on the off chance that there is one.

Establishing Consistent Routines and Schedules:

In the beginning phases of the sickness, day-to-day schedules assist people living with dementia in exploring their reality in an anticipated manner and adding a feeling of request to their days something that turns out to be considerably more significant as they lose consciousness of time. Additionally, since schedules are put away in long-term memory and dementia typically influences momentary memory first, schedules frequently stay open even into the center phases of illness.

Since they battle with momentary cognitive decline, individuals living with dementia find it challenging to learn better approaches for getting things done. They might battle to recall guidelines or to remain on track for an extended period of time. Everyday schedules help individuals with dementia adapt to these indications of momentary cognitive decline by drawing them into exercises that are natural. Since they realize they'll ultimately lose the capacity to do numerous ordinary undertakings, proceeding to do these things as far as might be feasible turns out to be particularly significant. It supports a feeling of freedom, constructs confidence, and might in fact assist them with holding abilities longer.

One more critical benefit of the everyday daily schedule for dementia patients is a decrease in tension. As the infection advances, individuals living with dementia will generally turn out to be progressively baffled by their deficiency of mental and actual capacities. Schedules can assist them with confronting the day with a more prominent feeling of harmony and security, which reduces fomentation and inconvenient ways of behaving.

No less significant is the way that laying out everyday schedules can assist with diminishing pressure for parental figures. By establishing a climate and schedule that are more unsurprising, days frequently go by all the more easily. Also, when the individual with dementia is less upset, there are more open doors for snapshots of happiness and association.

Incorporating Meaningful Activities:

Intentional commitment is conceivable through basic exercises. To figure out what exercises could be the most significant, consider the individual's occupation, what they appreciated doing, and what satisfied them. Continuously adjust exercises to fit the individual's versatility, correspondence level, and tangible abilities. In their everyday daily practice, incorporate physical (body development), mental (including thinking), and social exercises (connecting with others), yet additionally permit satisfactory time for unwinding. Plan short exercises. Individuals with dementia can find it difficult to maintain their concentration for quite a while.

Consider exercises that are animated and simple to follow.

- Plan exercises that include simple, monotonous activities and basic advances. Exercises with redundant activity are reasonable, in any event, for an individual with cutting-edge dementia.
- Give sufficient time between directions. Trust that the individual will finish a stage prior to giving the following guidance. Help if necessary, yet do not complete the action for them.
- Give close consideration to their response and do whatever it takes not to overwhelm them.

On the off chance that the individual loses interest, change the action, change to an alternate one, or have some time off. Keep in mind that it's fine assuming they may be more keen on taking action than getting the result. For instance, blending treat mixtures by hand may be a tomfoolery and animating movement for the individual, yet they might not have any desire to be engaged with the baking part.

Incorporating Familiar Objects and Music:

For individuals who battle with dementia, particularly Alzheimer's disease, music can assist with diminishing side effects, particularly nervousness or anxiety. Playing music or paying attention to your favorite music can likewise further develop memory, which can slow the progression of the illness.

Music is intently attached to our recollections and feelings. At the point when we hear a specific tune, we may re-experience recollections we share with that melody, similar to whenever we first hit the dance floor with somebody, a kid's initial steps, a graduation service, or other huge life-altering situations.

Around 50 "scrounge packs" have been gathered at Section Hospice's Focal Illinois office in Bloomington. A few sacks are being dispersed to regional nursing homes for occupants with dementia, and some are accessible to the home guardians of individuals with dementia.

"Rather than tossing your garbage out, you can involve it for a truly significant reason—assisting somebody with dementia," said Jill Hudson of Gridley, among Sections Hospice volunteers gathering scavenge packs the week before.

Dementia is a deficiency of cerebrum capability that influences memory, thinking, language, judgment, and conduct. The most well-known type is Alzheimer's disease.
Scrounging, likewise called looking for, occurs in mid-to-late-arrange dementia, fundamentally Alzheimer's illness, when an individual is searching for an individual item the person believes is lost or has been taken.

Chapter seven

Managing Challenging Dementia Behaviors

One of the significant difficulties of really focusing on a friend or family member with Alzheimer's or another dementia is adapting to the disturbing way of behaving and character changes that frequently happen. Forcefulness, fantasies, meandering, or eating or resting troubles can be disturbing and make your job as a guardian considerably more troublesome.

Anything issues you're managing, it's memorable vital that the individual with dementia is purposely easy. Frequently, your adored one's social issues are aggravated by their current circumstances, their failure to manage pressure, or their disappointed endeavors to convey.

Understanding the Triggers for Behaviors

By carving out the opportunity to investigate and consider the triggers that are causing the senior you care for to be vexed, you will probably comprehend how to more readily speak with them, anticipate future surprises, and make life somewhat simpler all together.

A few models here demonstrate these normal triggers to search for:

-A climate that is overpowering to their faculties (a spot is excessively clearly or excessively swarmed).
-Being encircled by an excessive number of new faces, including having such a large number of guardians all at once.
-An adjustment of climate (e.g., going to visit a spot they haven't been previously or making changes to their assisted living condo or suite).
-Being eager, parched, or needing a washroom.
-Having somebody approach excessively fast or from the side where their fringe vision may be impeded
-Being befuddled about their area and how they arrived (even in a once-natural climate).
-Having somebody talk too noisily or strongly to them
-At the point when individual space is attacked, whether it is by a companion or relative or something more odd when you are out in a public spot.
-Misconception bearings or inquiries from a friend or family member or a discussion that is happening close by.
-Being frightened by an uproarious commotion or by boisterous voices
- At the point when a climate is excessively blistering or excessively cold to settle in.
-Feeling disparaged or affronted by companions, family, or guardians.
-Low confidence is conveyed by a powerlessness and helps them really focus on themselves.

-Incidental effects from, association with, or antagonistic response to medications

Strategies for Calming Agitation and Restlessness

Fretfulness and tumult are normal ways of behaving for individuals living with dementia. These ways of behaving can be challenging for others to comprehend, yet figuring out the causes can assist you in supporting the individual. They might be a side effect of the actual changes in the mind brought about by dementia. An individual might become unsettled out of nowhere as a result of a change or explicit reason, for example, expanded clamor or not having the option to accomplish something they beforehand could. Or, on the other hand, they might feel a general sense of disturbance but not know why.

An individual with Alzheimer's might feel restless or disturbed. The person in question might become fretful, making a need to move around or pace, or become vexed in specific situations or when zeroed in on unambiguous subtleties.

Eventually, the individual with dementia will organically encounter a significant loss of their capacity to haggle new data and boost. It is an immediate consequence of the sickness.

Circumstances that might prompt tumult include:

- Moving to another home or nursing home
- Changes in climate, like travel, hospitalization, or the presence of houseguests
- Changes in parental plans
- Misperceived dangers
- Dread and exhaustion come about when attempting to figure out a confounding world.
- Treating social side effects. Anybody encountering social side effects ought to get a careful clinical exam, particularly when side effects show up out of nowhere. Treatment relies on a cautious conclusion, deciding potential causes and the kinds of conduct the individual is encountering. With legitimate treatment and mediation, the side effects of fomentation can be diminished.

Tips to assist with forestalling disturbances

To forestall or decrease unsettling:

- Establish a quiet climate. Eliminate stressors. This might mean moving the individual to a more secure or calmer spot or offering a security item, rest, or protection.

- Have a go at calming customs and restricting caffeine use.
- Keep away from ecological triggers.Commotion, glare, and foundation interruptions (for example, having the TV on) can act as triggers.Screen for individual solace.
- Check for torment, hunger, thirst, clogging, a full bladder, weakness, diseases, and skin irritation.
- Ensure the room is at an agreeable temperature.
- Be sensitive to fears, misperceived dangers, and dissatisfaction with communicating what is needed.
- Work on errands and schedules.
- Give yourself a valuable chance to work out. Take a walk. Garden together. Put on music and dance.

Dealing with Aggression and Irritability

Continuously examine worries about a forceful way of behaving with the individual's primary care physician. They can check for an actual ailment or inconvenience and give counsel. The specialist can likewise search for basic mental diseases or conceivable drug symptoms.

Know about a particular advance notice indication of hostility:

- Lessen or eliminate potential reasons for pressure.

73

- Attempt to maintain an unrushed and reliable daily practice.
- Keep the climate predictable and limit changes.
- Keep away from overwhelming conditions, for example, bunches of individuals or foundation commotion.
- Convey in a manner that matches the individual's capacity to comprehend and answer.
- Keep away from a showdown.
- Attempt interruptions or recommend an alternate movement.
- Empower normal activity and cooperation in charming exercises.
- Amplify sensations of solace and security.

In spite of your earnest attempts, some animosity might, in any case, happen.

Coping with Sundowning and Sleep Disturbances

The expression "sundowning" alludes to a mess happening in the late evening and enduring into the evening. Sundowning can cause various ways of behaving, like disarray, nervousness, hostility, or disregarding headings. Sundowning can likewise prompt pacing or meandering.

Sundowning isn't a sickness. A gathering of side effects happens at a particular time. These side effects might influence individuals with Alzheimer's illness and different sorts of dementia. The specific reason for this conduct is obscure.

Individuals with Alzheimer's and dementia might have issues dozing or increments in social issues that start at sunset and last into the evening (known as sundowning).
Evening anxiety doesn't endure forever. It normally tops in the center phases of Alzheimer's and afterward lessens as the sickness advances.

Here are some survival methods for rest issues and sundowning:

- Keep the home sufficiently bright at night. Satisfactory lighting might lessen the disturbance that happens when environmental elements are dull or new.

- Make an agreeable and safe rest climate: The individual's resting region ought to be at an agreeable temperature. Give nightlights and alternate ways of guarding the individual, for example, proper entryways and window locks. Entryway sensors and movement locators can be utilized to caution relatives when an individual is meandering.

- Keep a timetable: However much as could reasonably be expected, energize the individual with dementia to stick to an ordinary daily schedule of feasts, awakenings, and hitting the sack. This will take into consideration a more soothing rest around evening time.

- Stay away from energizers: Diminish or stay away from liquor, caffeine, and nicotine, which can all influence the capacity to rest. Put Sitting in front of the TV during times of alertness around evening time down, as it tends to animate.

- Plan more dynamic days: An individual who rests the greater part of the day is probably going to be conscious around evening time. Deter early evening snoozing and plan additional difficult exercises like medical checkups, excursions, and washing toward the beginning of the day or early evening. Support customary everyday workouts, however, no later than four hours before sleep time.

- Converse with a specialist: Examine unsettling influences with a specialist to assist with recognizing causes and potential arrangements. Most specialists energize the utilization of non-drug gauges instead of medicine.

Be aware of your own psychological and actual fatigue. In the event that you are feeling worried by the late evening, the individual might get on it and end up being fomented or befuddled. Attempt to get a lot of rest around evening time so you have more energy during the day.

Preventing Wandering and Ensuring Safety

Dementia meandering can be a risky occasion. The elderly can lose all sense of direction in hazardous spots, experience a fall and become harmed, or be exposed to a cruel climate. By rehearsing wellbeing measures, guardians can decrease the probability of meandering by more seasoned adults with dementia.

Alzheimer's illness and different types of dementia influence how the cerebrum functions. Two of the primary capacities dementia patients lose are late recollections and spatial review, which are basic for recalling areas. Seniors likewise experience issues reviewing why they left a particular region in any case.

Seniors with dementia might meander to get away from awkward boosts. As they leave, these maturing adults may fail to remember headings, face an obstacle on the arranged course, or understand that where they plan to travel is a fantasy of their creative mind or practically distant.

Chapter eight

Seeking Professional Support and Resources

Energize delicate touch when different types of correspondence appear to be troublesome. Holding the individual's hand, sitting with an arm around them, or even a delicate hand knead might be soothing for both the individual with dementia and their cherished one.

The Role of Medical Professionals in Dementia Care

Diagnosing, treating, and really focusing on individuals with Alzheimer's disease and related dementias are difficulties that require cooperation among relatives, clinical experts, other wellbeing specialist organizations, and networks. From there, the sky's the limit. Medical services experts are at the forefront of this work, working straightforwardly with patients and relatives. Learn more about the job of medical services experts in dementia care and about related central government assets and apparatuses.

Medical services experts are in many cases the primary resources for individuals with Alzheimer's or a connected dementia, including Lewy body dementia, vascular dementia, or frontotemporal dementia, who can assist with giving consideration and backing.

A few kinds of medical services experts might be associated with diagnosing and furnishing care to individuals with dementia. These include:

Essential consideration specialists:

- Nervous system specialists, who spend significant time on problems of the mind and sensory system
- Geriatricians, who represent considerable authority in the consideration of more seasoned adults
- Geriatric specialists, who spend significant time on the psychological and close-to-home soundness of more established adults
- Neuropsychologists, who have practical experience in normalized appraisal of cognizance and conduct
- Clinical clinicians, social laborers, and general therapists who have some expertise in grasping, diagnosing, and treating psychological wellness and conduct problems

Discourse, physical, and word-related advisors who spend significant time working on patients' capacity to impart and perform taking care of themselves exercises
- Attendants
- Home wellbeing associates

These experts might see patients at a wellness center, clinic, scholastic emergency clinic, or long-haul care office.

Medical services experts can provide different assets, including analytic assessments, therapy plans, instructive materials, and references to trained professionals, and that's just the beginning. Giving assets that emphasize dementia and dementia care is basic for further developing medical services, personal satisfaction, and generally results for individuals living with Alzheimer's and related dementias, as well as concerning their families and other consideration suppliers.

Enlisting the Help of Support Groups

The physical and close-to-home requests of really focusing on somebody with dementia can be high. In the event that you are really focusing on an individual with dementia, you may likewise require support so you can take care of yourself. It is more straightforward to proceed with your consideration job, assuming you get some down time to re-energize.

Associations and gatherings can help and support you, assuming that you are really focusing on somebody with dementia.
There are many spots that offer assets and backing for individuals with dementia and their guardians. These include: local area assets, for example, religious

associations; your neighborhood on Maturing; and nearby sections of the Alzheimer's Association.

Counselling and Therapy for Caregivers

Caregivers Gathering treatment is commonly shown to an expert specialist or qualified guide with explicit preparation in bunch treatment. They guide the gathering of guardians through various exercises and activities. These assist with people in the gathering to construct trust as they find out about one another's sentiments and difficulties.

Assistive Devices and Technology for Dementia Care

Assistive innovation, or dementia innovation, alludes to gadgets and frameworks that help an individual living with dementia finish the responsibilities of day-to-day living. These gadgets and gear can assist an individual with versatility and feebleness difficulties and issues with memory connected with their dementia.
Innovation in dementia care has been quickly developing as of late. Assistive innovation goes from savvy frameworks for your home to cautions to remind you to do specific undertakings through to cell phone applications that can give specialized apparatuses to dementia.

There are various ways in which assistive innovation can help an individual with dementia capitalize on life. Assistive innovation gadgets for dementia can assist with further developing security and freedom, yet they can likewise assist with observing wellbeing and prosperity.

Explicitly assistive innovation can assist with:

Memory challenges
Backing to design specific undertakings of regular day-to-day existence
Portability and development
Staying safe both throughout the homeCorrespondence (discourse and hearing)Socialization
Working on fearlessness and freedom

Here we list the sorts of gadgets and ready frameworks that can help an individual live well with dementia:

Versatile cell phones

Versatile cell phone innovation is progressively being utilized by more established individuals to deal with their lives and stay associated with friends and family. They permit you to settle on decisions and send instant messages, as well as empower you to utilize email and applications.

There are multiple ways they can be utilized as specialized instruments for dementia and assist an individual with keeping up with freedom:
Most versatile cell phones show a period and date, or the schedule capability can be utilized. Cautions can be set on the telephone to remind you to embrace an undertaking at a specific opportunity in the day. You can utilize it to get to other assistive innovations for dementia, for instance, in-home cameras, indoor regulators to set the temperature at home, and media administrations, for example, TV program planning. They can assist your loved one with the following of clinic or GP arrangements in the schedule capability, so they are reminded at a great time. Most associations presently use message suggestions to advise patients of flexible arrangements. Web-based shopping should be possible on portable cell phones, and sites that they visit routinely can be saved in a 'top picks' record. They can be utilized as security gadgets for dementia patients, guaranteeing they can continuously contact somebody in a crisis or that they need your help.

Timekeepers and Cautions

Not every person will feel okay with cell phone innovation. There are a few radio-controlled and computerized LCD tickers accessible. These have huge digits, so they are not difficult to see. There are a few tickers and gadgets that recognize whether it is morning, evening, or night through visual portrayal or the utilization of light. This is exceptionally useful to people who are living with dementia, as they in some cases battle to grasp the seasons of the day and may confound constantly.

GPS beacons

GPS beacons are the ideal security gadgets for dementia patients who may, on occasion, meander. The GPS beacon is worn by the individual residing with dementia, and the ready framework will raise a caution to a relative in the event that they have moved out of a specific region; for instance, they have gone out. They give relatives the much-required inner harmony that their cherished one is protected by.

Shrewd Gadgets

Shrewd gadgets like Amazon Reverberation, Google Home, and Apple HomePod can uphold an individual residing with dementia who is encountering issues with memory. These voice-enacted gadgets can set suggestions to inform your loved one when to get done with specific responsibilities, for instance, taking medicine. You can likewise ask them, for instance, what the date and time are. On the off chance that your loved one is OK with this innovation, they can request a shopping rundown to be made or for it to record a TV program utilizing further developed highlights. You would obviously have to have Wi-Fi set up in the home to utilize these highlights.

Electronic Machine Checking Gadget

In the event that you don't live with your cherished one, realizing they are protected will be of foremost significance to you. Another piece of innovation screens the utilization of electrical machines in the home, so you are cautioned when an apparatus is on and when it is off. In this way, on the off chance that they have left the cooker on for a delayed period, you will be told and can answer fittingly.

CAMERAS IN THE HOME
Introducing cameras in your cherished one's house is one more extraordinary method for guaranteeing their security while giving you consolation. Numerous gadgets can then be connected to an application on your cell phone, so you can see precisely the way in which your cherished one is, wherever you are.

ELECTRONIC Prescriptions
The boardThere is a huge scope of computerized pill containers and boxes available. They give caution to remind those living with dementia or their family caregivers that the time has come to take medicine. A few containers can be connected to a vibrating caution on a watch. This innovation implies that drugs can be administered securely and effectively for those living with dementia.

Enormous Picture Telephones

Many individuals living with dementia battle to remember telephone numbers and may have to reach out to somebody rapidly or in a crisis. These telephones have enormous number fasteners and are customized with regularly called numbers.

A few telephones have clear fasteners where photographs of their relatives are on a button that would then dial that individual in the event that they were required.

There are a couple of things you really want to consider while picking assistive innovation for dementia patients. You might wish to consider talking with a Word-related specialist to get their recommendation on what gear would best address your loved one's issues. They will lead a complete evaluation of their requirements and how they wish to carry on with their lives, as well as examine with the family their perspectives on what might make life simpler.

It is consistently essential to guarantee your cherished one is taken part in the thing being anticipated of them, so their decisions and wishes are respected. It is possible that your cherished one isn't happy utilizing imaginative innovation and will require help and support to bring it into their lives. No choice ought to be made that confines an individual's opportunity or protection.

Contingent upon where they are in their dementia process, some innovation may not be suitable, and it can never supplant balanced care given by a family or expert caregiver, assuming that is what your cherished one necessities. It is actually significant that dementia innovation ought to never supplant close and personal contact to remain associated with adored ones'.

This could unfavorably affect an individual's general prosperity and may make them feel socially separated.

Here are a few things you might wish to consider while picking assistive innovation for dementia:
- Whether there is a requirement for it or could you at any point get the help another way
- What innovation will best address your issues?Your inclinations and capacity to utilize gadgets, and how these could change after some time
- Whether you have any other circumstances that might influence how you utilize the innovation (like sight or hearing issues),The amount of help you possess from others and whether you can require this to utilize the innovation
- How well the innovation will find a place with your standard schedules
- Whether the innovation requires a telephone line or web access, the expense of the innovation

Chapter nine

Practical Tips for Everyday Dementia Care

Alzheimer's infection and related dementias deteriorate over the long run. Indeed, even straightforward, regular exercises can become hard to finish. To help adapt to changes in memory and thinking, consider methodologies that can make everyday assignments simpler. Attempt to embrace them from the get-go so you will have additional opportunity to change.

Assisting with Daily Living Activities

Investing energy with a relative or companion in the early or late phases of Alzheimer's can be significant and fun, particularly if you follow the individual. What do they get a kick out of the chance to do? What are they ready to do? What is their mindset for now? The following are a couple of thoughts to get everything rolling!

1. Outside exercises

2. Indoor exercises

3. Individual exercises

4. Kitchen exercises

Accomplish something outside

- Family going for a stroll in the forest, granddad holding grandkids' hands.
- Go for a stroll.
- Plant blossoms water plants
- Feed the birds.
- Rake leavesGo to the recreation area.
- Sit on a seat or a swing.
- Guard dogs at a canine park
- Play catch or throw a ball.
- Play horseshoes
- Visit an oceanside or backwoods reserve.
- Clear the yard or deck.
- Set up a cookout in the yard or on the patio.
- Sit in the yard and drink espresso, hot cocoa, or lemonade.

Accomplish something inside

- Family playing Uno
- Pay attention to the individual's #1 music.
- Check out the family photograph collections.
- Get ready for evening tea.
- Watch the most loved sport on TV.
- Model with a play mixture
- Play checkers or dominoes.

- Name the presidents.
- Take a gander at photographs in a photography book or magazine.
- Distinguish states on a U.S. map
- Complete a riddle together.
- Peruse one of their #1 book.
- Watch a most-loved film or sitcom.
- Watch a game
- Get some information about their experience growing up, kin, school, pets, or first vehicle.
- Peruse the paper together or read it to them.
- Play a game.

Accomplish something individual

- Give the individual a hand rub with a salve.
- Brush their hair.
- Give the individual a nail treatment.
- Take photographs of the individual and make a collection.
- Urge the individual to discuss subjects they appreciate.
- Make a genealogical record banner board.

Accomplish something in the kitchen

A more seasoned lady is embracing the young lady and giving her a lunch plate.

- Heat treats or bread. Put everything on the table.
- Make the individual's #1 lunch or tidbit
- Wash and dry dishes.
- Set flatware aside.
- Celebrate family occasions and customs.
- Pay attention to popular event music.
- Heat-occasion pastries Variety eggs
- Cut a pumpkin or make a pumpkin pie.
- Enhance a tree
- Make occasion welcoming cards.
- Watch a most-loved occasion film
- Play a piano or guitar and sing occasional tunes.

It doesn't make any difference assuming that the movement should be finished, or, on the other hand, if it gets along admirably. In the event that it doesn't work, you can constantly take a stab at something different. Be patient, and you will sort out what works.

Ensuring Proper Nutrition and Hygiene

Sustenance assumes a significant role in dementia care in light of multiple factors. Appropriate sustenance is fundamental in dementia care to keep up with mental capability, forestall ailing health and parchedness, and work on, generally speaking, personal satisfaction.

Individuals with dementia, first and foremost, may experience issues eating or planning feasts for themselves because of their mental and actual weaknesses. This can prompt unhealthiness and drying out, which can deteriorate mental capability and, by and large, wellbeing.

Individuals with dementia might encounter changes in their taste and cravings, which can make it difficult to guarantee that they are getting satisfactory nourishment. So it's truly essential to offer different supplement-rich food sources that are engaging and simple to eat.

As well as giving legitimate nourishment, parental figures can likewise carry out ways of advancing smart dieting propensities in individuals with dementia, for example, making a daily practice for dinners, offering little and regular feasts over the course of the day, and giving help eating if necessary.

Encouraging Physical Activity and Exercise

Certain individuals with dementia will most likely be unable to get around well. This is another issue that turns out to be more difficult to manage as the sickness deteriorates.

A few potential purposes behind this include:

- Issues with perseverance
- Unfortunate coordination
- Sore feet or muscles

- Ailment
- Melancholy or general indifference

Regardless of whether individuals experience difficulty strolling, they might have the option to:

- Do basic errands around the home, like clearing and cleaning.
- Utilise an exercise bike.
- Utilise delicate elastic activity balls or inflatables for extending or tossing this way and that.
- Use extending groups, which you can purchase in outdoor supply stores.
- Make certain to adhere to the guidelines.
- Lift loads or family things, for example, soup jars.

Engaging in Meaningful Social Connections

Social association impacts our brains, bodies, and ways of behaving, all of which impact our wellbeing and future. Research demonstrates the way that social connectedness can prompt a longer life, better wellbeing, and prosperity.

Social connectedness is how much individuals have and see an ideal number, quality, and variety of connections that give them the feeling of having a place and being really focused on, esteemed, and upheld.

Individuals are essentially friendly animals. Social associations are significant for our endurance. Our associations with family, companions, collaborators, and local area individuals can significantly affect our wellbeing and prosperity.

At the point when individuals are socially associated and have steady and strong connections, they are bound to settle on sound decisions and to have better mental and actual wellbeing results. They are additionally better prepared to adapt to difficult situations, stress, tension, and misery.

There are numerous things that contribute to social connectedness. The sum and nature of our connections matter, as do the different jobs they play in our lives.

Chapter ten

Embracing Compassionate Love: Stories from Caregivers

A caregiver of Alzheimer's and dementia patients was asked what "best examples" they would impart to a companion or partner who is new to Alzheimer's or dementia care. Here was her reaction.

Marie is newer to being an Alzheimer's guardian, as her dad was determined to have mid-stage Alzheimer's just last year. He and Marie's mom live with Marie, her significant other, and their young girl. Marie and her significant other both work all day; her typical business day begins at 6 a.m., his at 2 p.m., and Marie's mom works part-time. These timetables permit one of them to constantly be with her dad, which became fundamental following his new meandering episode.

Through tears, Marie communicated her mind-boggling sensations of culpability, responsibility for being irate with him for having this illness, culpability for being furious that his conduct makes their lives more troublesome, and culpability when she wishes things were the way they used to be. She has taken classes to all the more likely figure out the infection, and she says she sometimes peruses online guardian remarks relating to the blameworthy sentiments individuals express. Up to this point, however, she has not had the option to determine these sensations of culpability. She stays disappointed, furious, and tired, and she truly regrets not yet having the option to acknowledge things as they are. She didn't know she had an "example" to offer. I advised her that culpability is ordinary, and by doing what she is doing, taking classes and perusing the web-based gatherings, she is doing all she can right now to acknowledge it.

Real-Life Experiences and Insights

Absence of knowledge is connected with loss of action in regions toward the front of an individual's cerebrum (known as the cerebrums). It is more considered normal in certain kinds of dementia that are connected to harm in this part of the mind, for example, frontotemporal dementia (FTD). Yet, an individual with dementia can have an absence of understanding.

Lessons Learned from Compassionate Caregivers

1. Care accomplices are guardians of someone else's gallery of life.
2. The natural worth and nobility of individuals can't be taken away by any condition or situation. With empathy, we should initially accept that all individuals have an indisputable character.

3. The magnificence, imperativeness, and social energies inside the extreme one living with dementia can give motivation to the consideration of an accomplice's excursion.

4. We ought to adore and respect people in their present status, as opposed to considering them responsible to be what our self-images need them to be.

5. Permit people living with dementia the chance to communicate their thoughts as totally as possible.

6. Interruptions should be limited during cooperation with people who are living with dementia.

7. We ought to continuously look at individuals without flinching when they are sharing their accounts. We ought to understand that they might be sharing their accounts without using words.

8. One's story needs to emerge. At the point when words fall flat, craftsmanship in all structures can be a vehicle for communicating one's story. Expressive expressions and potential chances to investigate imagination ought to be made accessible to every individual who is living with dementia.

9. Nothing mixes the spirit in excess of the sensation of having a place. We should do everything possible to advance this sort of involvement day to day in individuals who are living with dementia.

10. Continuously attempt to recollect the quiet battles of others, which might lie covered underneath mentalities and ways of behaving of which we don't have any idea.

Inspiring Examples of Compassionate

Empathy displayed toward my grandma is my motivation.Jayde Currie, an understudy nurse, has been a youthful caregiver for the vast majority of her life, assisting with taking care of her mom, who experiences weakness and dysfunctional behavior; her sister, who likewise has psychological instabilities; and afterward, her grandma, who has dementia. Here she recollects the last long periods of Jessie Logan Dempster and the altruistic consideration she got both in the emergency clinic and at home.

Last December, my 83-year-old grandmother, Jessie, was taken into the clinic. She had dementia and was enduring incoherence, so everything was terrifying to her. She didn't have the foggiest idea who the men contacting her were; she didn't see the reason why she was lying in a bed and unfit to move since she was so powerless; and most importantly, she truly failed to see the reason why individuals (who she knew were her family, yet didn't exactly have the foggiest idea how they were family) were crying as the emergency vehicle men persuaded her to be taken into a medical clinic.
She was confused on the grounds that she was sure she was not yet a little kid. At the point when it began to get dim, she got energized on the grounds that her daddy was expected home and consistently brought her darlings. She used to attempt to get up to get the transport or would have been behind schedule for work.

She would visit my sisters and me as though we were only her companions, educating us regarding moving and other superb things she got up to in her life as a youngster.

So when she got taken into the medical clinic, our entire house changed: there was nobody staying there standing by to offer their viewpoint on an outfit for an evening out on the town, nobody requesting that you drive the whole way to the nearest chippy to get a piece of squanders. Despite the fact that dementia had removed all that we had known about our "old" grandmother, we then developed to adore our "new" one.

Yet, her visit to the Crosshouse clinic caused me to acknowledge how glad and favored I'm to prepare next to NHS Ayrshire and Arran attendants, clinical staff, and a host of other people who have an effect on our patients. Everything was finished to ensure my grandmother was cheerful, agreeable, and content; she even assisted with enjoying her last Christmas with her loved ones.

At the point when she came home at last in January, she got palliative consideration from the local nurture that will remain with me for eternity. They were sympathetic and merciful, and despite the fact that she was presently not ready to answer, they talked her through each step of her consideration, talking as though she could answer. They respected her privileges and her viewpoints.

I trust one day I can make NHS Ayrshire and Arran as pleased as they ought to be with the medical attendants engaged with my grandmother's consideration. I'm energetic about caring for patients with dementia and maintain that one day I should spend significant time on it. This experience has provided a motivating illustration of what a medical caretaker ought to be.

Love in Dementia Care

Individuals with dementia need to feel cherished, to have a good sense of reassurance, and to feel acknowledged. Cherishing contact and fondness from their companions can present to them a ton of solace and try and assist with decreasing a portion of the negative conduct and mental side effects of dementia.

All couples confronting dementia should track down better approaches to sustain and advance their closeness, and commonly, the parental figure's life partner is the person who bears the best portion of the obligation regarding keeping the relationship alive. This is a repetitive point in discussions among companion parental figures, who, in the care groups they join in, frequently trade important data and survival techniques on how they save their relationship all through the movement of dementia.

In a general sense, all techniques for improving correspondence between companions might possibly assist with advancing closeness and saving the relationship. There are various projects and studios accessible for couples impacted by dementia that are planned to build interchange and harmony. Programs that animate correspondence between mates through shared creative articulation, including visual expressions, melodies, and body work, are especially useful.

Some dementia-related side effects that might be influencing the relationship can be tended to and eased with appropriate clinical treatment. Life partner parental figures ought to be urged to examine relationship challenges with the specialist and look for conceivable treatment choices.

Chapter eleven

Conclusion

All in all, we realize that dementia has to do with the deficiency of memory and other reasoning abilities and can abbreviate an individual's skill. Dementia influences an individual's day-to-day existence, from preparing supper to driving a vehicle. We realize that this problem is certainly not a particular sickness and that there is no known fix except for prescriptions, which can briefly further develop side effects. Subsequently, any harm done to the synapses (neurons) is irreversible. We discovered that this sickness is like a vascular illness.7 Alzheimer's sickness, and lewy body illness. We discovered that a horrendous mishap to the head may likewise cause dementia and AIDS at a prior age. We realize there are hereditary qualities included, but there is no reasonable example of a legacy that can be recognized. We discovered that 5,000,000 individuals in the U.S. are impacted and that women have a higher risk of getting dementia than men. Besides, men will quite often be more forceful and backward than women. Ladies will generally show more ways of behaving in misery and fantasies, where men don't. We investigated medicines for dementia and observed that men with dementia are typically recommended antipsychotics, while ladies are endorsed antidepressants. In particular, we discovered that this sickness can influence anybody and that loved ones should make arrangements when such occurs.

Recap of Key Points

Dementia is the deficiency of mental working, thinking, recalling, and thinking so much that it obstructs an individual's everyday existence and exercises. Certain individuals with dementia have no control over their feelings, and their characters might change. Dementia ranges in seriousness from the mildest stage, when it is simply starting to influence an individual's work, to the most extreme stage, when the individual should rely totally upon others for essential exercises of day-to-day living, like taking care of oneself.

10 Encouraging Quotes for Caregivers

Statements of the day
1. "Thoughtfulness can change somebody's dim second with a blast of light. You won't ever know how much your mindfulness issues are."
2. "Despite the challenge you are confronting at present, realize that it has not come to remain. It has happened. During these times, give your very best for what you have and request help if necessary. Above all, I won't ever give up. Put things in context. Deal with yourself. Track down ways of renewing your energy, reinforce your

confidence, and brace yourself from the back to the front."
3. "There are just four sorts of individuals on the planet: the individuals who have been guardians. The people who are right now parental figures The individuals who will be parental figures and the people who will require a guardian
4. "Being profoundly adored by somebody invigorates you, while cherishing somebody profoundly gives you boldness."
5. "They might fail to remember what you said, yet they will always remember how you affected them.
6. "Providing care frequently calls us to incline toward adoration we didn't know was imaginable."
7. "A decent chuckle and an extended rest are the two best solutions for anything."
8. "My parental figure mantra is to remember: the main control you have is over the progressions you decide to make."
9. "To really focus on the people who once focused on us is perhaps the greatest honor."
10. "To cherish an individual is to see the entirety of their wizardry and to help them remember it when they have neglected it."